GW01326435

COOKBOOK
FOR CHILDREN

Cookbook for children

by
Monica Badelt and
Ingrid Nijkerk

CHESHIRE
LIBRARIES AND MUSEUMS
14 DEC 1990
ASW K 0155

WITHDRAWN

© MCMLXXXIV by Zuidnederlandse Uitgeverij N.V.
Aartselaar.
All rights reserved.
© MCMLXXXV Invader Ltd.,
10 Eastgate Square, Chichester, England.
All rights reserved. No part of this publication may be repro-
duced, stored in a retrieval system or transmitted, in any
form or by any means, electronic, mechanical, photocopying,
recording or otherwise, without the prior permission of the
copyright owner.
ISBN 1-85129-076-1
Printed in Belgium.

Foreword

Children love to do their own cooking. Some of the books that have been produced for children assume that they have a basic knowledge of cookery. COOKBOOK FOR CHILDREN starts with the most basic instructions and shows step by step how the recipes should be prepared. Each step is simplified by an illustration, so that the children see how the stages of preparation, as well as the finished dish, should look.
COOKBOOK FOR CHILDREN also gives practical information and advice on kitchen equipment and procedures.

Important things to know

Cooking and preparing tasty things can be great fun. Before you start to work in the kitchen, you must always wash your hands thoroughly, even if you are going to get them dirty again cleaning vegetables for example. If your hands get dirty, make a habit of washing them again straight away. This way, you keep the kitchen utensils clean as well as the food you are preparing. The cleaner you keep everything, the better you can work.

First, decide what you want to make. Read the recipe right through and get everything ready in the way of utensils and ingredients, so that you don't have to start looking for these while you are cooking. Make sure you have enough space left to work! The ingredients should be arranged in order of use and not mixed up in a pile or left so that they can get spilt. Put things that you have used and won't need anymore back were they belong in the cupboard, as soon as you can. It is very useful to have a washing-up bowl and suds ready so that you can wash up and put away the utensils that aren't needed anymore. This saves a lot of cleaning up afterwards... Mum will be very impressed!

Take care that sharp tools, like knives, don't fall on the ground or on your feet. If you need to cut or chop something always use a chopping board, preferably on top of a damp cloth on the draining board. This will stop the board sliding and perhaps cutting your fingers.

If you have to light gas, first strike the match and then turn the gas switch slowly to medium whilst keeping the lighted match close to the burner. If you turned the gas to the highest flame straight away, it could flare up and burn you or the match could get blown out by the force of the gas. If you are working with an electric cooker or an electric burner, remember that these may need time to heat up. Also, the rate of cooling off varies with different cookers and you have to be careful when cooking things like soup or porridge that can easily boil over. Once you have cooked a few times with electricity, you usually know how long it takes to heat up or cool down, but in the beginning it is sensible to ask your mother to show you.

Never work with pans that are too heavy for you when full. This can be very dangerous if you have to lift the pans off the heat. Of course, you must turn off the heat before you lift off a pan. You should hold the pan with oven gloves or an oven cloth. Don't be too hasty, make sure the heat doesn't come through anywhere. If you don't check this you could drop the pan and spill the hot contents over yourself.

So always pay attention to everything you do in the kitchen, it all needs some thought beforehand. Don't rush anything. Concentrate on everything you do. Don't let yourself be distracted by talking to your sister of a friend, and make sure there is somewhere safe to put the hot pan when you take it off the heat.

It is a very good idea to use a large bucket lined with a plastic bag and immediately discard all refuse and rubbish, potato peelings, vegetable refuse and packaging materials into it. This saves a lot of time clearing up afterwards and keeps the working area tidy. So, when you present the dish you have prepared *and* the kitchen is spotless... Mum will be very impressed!!

Things you need in the kitchen

A stewpan or casserole
A deep pan for soup, vegetables, etc, with a lid and two handles.

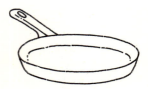

A frying pan
This is used for cooking food quickly. That is why this pan is usually more heat-resistant than ordinary pans, and should have a heavy base.

A saucepan
Saucepans can be used to stir sauces, heat soup or porridge and boil liquids such as milk.

A colander
Ingredients can be strained through a colander or rinsed in it.

A measuring jug
A measuring jug is used to measure quantities of ingredients. Usually, the measurements for dry goods (sugar, flour) are on one side and the liquid measurements (milk, water) are on the other side.

A mixing bowl
A large, deep bowl for mixing.

A cup
A cup can be used to stir cornflour or flour to blend with sauces or puddings. It is also sometimes used for measuring.

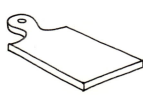

A chopping board
A chopping board can be used for slicing vegetables or for chopping cheese or meat.

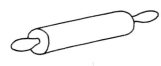

A rolling pin
A rolling pin dusted with flour is used to roll pastry dough into flat pieces. In this way the pastry becomes smooth and even.

A sieve
A sieve can be used to sift flour. It can be used to puree fruit by pressing it through the sieve. Soup can be put through a sieve to remove bones, etc.

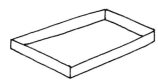

A baking tray or tin
On this tin with raised edges, you can bake biscuits but also flat cakes like shortbread. It can be lined with a sheet of aluminium foil to keep it clean when baking.

A mould
The mould is used for jellies or puddings.

An egg whisk
A whisk is used for beating cream, egg or mayonnaise. It can also be used to mix porridge to prevent lumps forming.

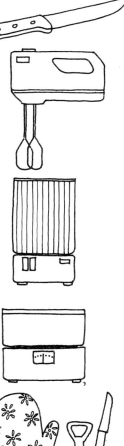

A meat knife
A meat knife can be a dangerous tool. If the knife in your kitchen is very big, it is preferable to use a smaller knife for slicing. Ask Mum to help you if you're worried about using a sharp knife.

An electric mixer
A faster method of whisking or beating.

A mixer-blender
This machine can mix milkshakes, etc. as well as blend ingredients together.

Scales
This is for weighing ingredients which are needed in a recipe.

Odds and ends
Potato knife, corkscrew, bottle opener, oven gloves.

egg dishes

Boiled egg

1 Put an egg into a tablespoon and place it in a pan of boiling water.

2 Boil for 4 mins. for a soft-boiled egg and 10 mins. for a hard-boiled egg.

Omelette

1 Break 2 or 3 eggs into a bowl, add a tablespoon of milk and a pinch of salt.

3 Put a tablespoon of butter into a pan and put this on the heat.

2 Stir the mixture thoroughly with a fork.

4 Pour the egg mixture into the pan and fry for 4 to 5 mins then carefully tip out on to a plate.

Fried egg

1 Put a teaspoon of butter into the frying pan and put this on the heat.

2 Break the egg into a cup and then let it slide out of the cup into the pan. Fry gently for 4 to 5 mins and then serve at once.

15

You will need: 6 slices stale white bread
3 eggs
about 100 g/4 oz butter
1/2 cup milk

french toast

1 Put 3 eggs into a dish and whisk together.

2 Add the milk.

3 Soak the bread in the eggs and milk.

4 Put a tablespoon of butter into the pan and leave it to melt.

5 Put the bread into the pan and fry on both sides until golden brown.

6 Put the bread on a plate and sprinkle with sugar or spread with jam.

You will need:
100 g/4 oz soft butter
125 g/4 oz fine sugar (castor sugar)
1 egg
200 g/7 oz flour

1 Heat oven to 180°C/350°F/ Gas mark 4. Stir the butter and sugar together in a bowl until it is a creamy mixture.

2 Beat the egg in a small bowl or cup.

3 Stir the egg into the butter and sugar mixture.

4 Pour the flour through the sieve into the mixing bowl, and stir everything together very thoroughly.

5 Sprinkle the table with flour. Roll out the dough with the rolling pin to a thickness of about 5 cm/2".

6 Press out shapes with biscuit cutters.

7 Decorate the shapes with chocolate bits, raisins or a tiny blob of jam.

8 Bake biscuits for about 10 to 15 mins.

You will need for 4 people: 4 tomatoes / 4 eggs / about 50 g/2 oz butter / breadcrumbs / salt and pepper

eggs in tomatoes

1 Heat the oven to about 220°C/430°F/Gas mark 7.

2 Wash the tomatoes and dry them well.

3 Slice the top off each tomato, hollow them out with a spoon and season the inside with salt and pepper.

4 Grease an ovenproof dish with butter and then place the tomatoes in it.

5 Break an egg into a cup and let it slide into one of the tomatoes, do the same with the other tomatoes.

6 Sprinkle a little salt and pepper on to the egg. Sprinkle with breadcrumbs and finally put a dab of butter on top.

7 Put the dish into the oven and bake until the egg white is set, about 20 mins.

8 Serve immediately.

You will need for 4 people:
8 slices of bread
4 slices of cheese
4 large slices of ham
about 100 g/4 oz butter

croque-monsieur

1 Remove the crusts from the bread.

2 Butter the slices of bread on one side.

3 Place the cheese on the 4 buttered slices of bread.

4 Now place the ham on the cheese.

5 Place the other 4 slices of bread on top.

6 Melt a little butter in a pan on a low heat.

7 Fry the croque-monsieur gently on both sides until it is golden brown.

8 Make sure that the cheese is well melted.

You will need: about 50 g/2 oz cooking chocolate
                  2 eggs
                  2 tablespoons icing sugar

chocolate mousse

1 Break the chocolate into a bowl.

2 Fill a saucepan about half full with water and bring it to the boil.

3 Carefully place the bowl with the chocolate into the hot water.

4 When the chocolate is melted, take the pan off the heat.

5 Separate the egg whites from the yolks and put into separate bowls. Beat the egg whites with the icing sugar until stiff.

6 Beat the egg yolks a little and then add them to the melted chocolate.

7 Stir the beaten egg whites very carefully into the chocolate.

8 Put the chocolate mousse into dessert bowls and leave to stand for 1 hour in a cool place.

You will need: 300 g/10 oz spaghetti
a pinch of salt, pepper
2 tablespoons oil
½ tin peeled tomatoes or
3 fresh peeled tomatoes

½ teaspoon oregano
2 heaped tablespoons grated cheese
1 tablespoon butter
1 onion, sliced

spaghetti with tomato sauce

1 Pour 3 litres/5½ pints of water into a large pan, add a pinch of salt and bring to the boil.

2 Put the spaghetti with the oil into the boiling water. Cook according to the instructions on the packet.

3 Finely chop the onion. Melt the butter in a saucepan, add the onion and fry until brown.

4 Add the tomatoes to the onion.

5 Season with oregano, pepper and salt and leave everything to cook for about 10 mins.

6 Drain the spaghetti in a colander.

7 Pour the spaghetti into a serving dish and pour the tomato sauce over the top.

8 Sprinkle the grated cheese on top of the sauce and serve.

You will need
for 4 people:
4 large sour apples
2 tablespoons butter
4 teaspoons brown sugar
4 teaspoons white sugar

apples in the oven

1 Heat the oven to 220°C/430°F/Gas mark 7.

2 Wash the apples and dry them well.

3 Remove the core, perhaps it's better if your mother helps you with this.

4 Take a pointed knife and make six cuts in the top half of the apple.

5 Put the apples into an ovenproof dish.

6 Stir together the butter and brown sugar, and spoon this into the apples.

7 Sprinkle the apples with the white sugar.

8 Put the apples into the oven and bake for 35 mins.

You will need
for 4 people:
1 packet of frozen flaky pastry
4 sausages
1 egg yolk

sausage rolls

1 Thaw out the flaky pastry.

2 Heat the oven to 220°C/430°F/Gas mark 7.

3 Roll out the pastry with a rolling pin to about ⅓ cm/¼" thickness.

4 Cut the pastry into 4 equal pieces.

5 Brush the sides of the pastry pieces with a little water.

6 Roll up a sausage in each piece of pastry and place it on a baking tray.

7 Spread the top of each sausage roll with a little egg yolk.

8 Bake for about 20 mins. and then serve at once.

apple pie

You will need:

150 g/5 oz butter or margarine
150 g/5 oz sugar
250 g/8 oz self raising flour
1 egg, lightly beaten
a pinch of salt

For the filling:
about 50 g/2 oz raisins
about 50 g/2 oz sugar
about 500 g/1lb sour apples
2 tablespoons breadcrumbs
coarse sugar

1 Heat the oven to about 150°C/300°F/Gas mark 2.

2 Knead together the flour, butter, sugar, salt and half of the egg to make a pastry mixture.

3 Roll out the pastry and put into a buttered pie tin, keeping a little of the pastry aside.

4 Sprinkle the base of the pie with breadcrumbs.

5 Peel and core the apples and cut them into not too thick wedges.

6 Put them into a bowl with the raisins, sugar and some cinnamon. Spread them over the pastry.

7 Using the remaining pastry, cut out narrow strips to make a lattice work across the pie.

8 Brush the pie with the rest of the egg yolk and sprinkle coarse sugar over the top. Bake for about 50-60 mins.

You will need: 150 g/5 oz self raising flour
150 g/5 oz soft butter or margarine
150 g/5 oz sugar
3 eggs

a pinch of salt
2 drops vanilla essence
1 tablespoon breadcrumbs

cake

1 Heat the oven to about 160°C/325°F/Gas mark 3.

2 Stir the soft butter together with the vanilla essence, sugar and salt until it is a creamy mixture.

3 Add the eggs one by one and beat the mixture for several minutes.

4 Sieve the flour and mix it in carefully.

5 Grease the cake tin and sprinkle the sides with breadcrumbs to prevent the cake from sticking. Pour in the cake mixture.

6 Bake for about 50-60 mins. until golden brown.

7 The cake is ready if you can stick a knitting needle into it and draw it out clean.

8 Leave the cake to cool for another 10-15 mins. before removing it from the tin.

You will need: 1 packet vanilla pudding or custard
600 ml/1 pint milk
4-5 heaped tablespoons sugar
1 small tin fruit salad
cream

pudding with fruit

1 Put the powder into a cup and stir in 4 tablespoons of cold milk.

2 Add sugar to the rest of the milk and bring to the boil in a small saucepan.

3 Take the pan off the heat as soon as the milk begins to boil.

4 Stir the cup of dissolved mixture into the hot milk. Put the pan back on the heat. Simmer and keep stirring until the mixture thickens.

5 Rinse 4 glass dessert bowls with water and pour in the pudding.

6 Leave them to cool in the refrigerator.

7 Drain the fruit salad and distribute it over the cooled puddings.

8 Serve with cream.

You will need for 2 people:

1 lemon
2 bananas
2 oranges
1 pear
1 apple

some grapes
2 half peaches out of a tin
(or any other seasonal fruit)
2 drops vanilla essence
3 heaped tablespoons of sugar

fruit salad

1 Squeeze the lemon.

2 Bring the lemon juice, sugar and vanilla essence to the boil very briefly in a small saucepan.

3 Peel the bananas, apple, oranges, grapes and the pear and cut everything into small pieces.

4 Mix the fruit well to prevent the apple and the pear becoming brown.

5 Cut the peaches into small pieces.

6 Mix well with the fresh fruit in a bowl and cover all the fruit with the syrup.

7 Leave the bowl to stand for 1-2 hours in the refrigerator.

8 Serve with cream or icecream.

You will need: 1 packet frozen flaky pastry   200 g/7 oz grated cheese
1 tablespoon olive oil   salt and black pepper
400 g/14 oz tin of tomatoes   1 teaspoon dried oregano

pizza

1 Thaw the pastry.

2 Heat the oven to 220°C/425°F/Gas mark 7.

3 Roll the pastry out thinly and lay it in a pizza dish.

4 Cut off the overlapping edges.

5 Drain the tomatoes and arrange them on the pastry.

6 Sprinkle the tomatoes with salt, pepper and dried oregano.

7 Distribute the cheese evenly over the pizza.

8 Bake for about 20 mins. in the oven and then serve at once.

Some good ideas

On hot days when nobody feels like eating a hot meal, little vegetable snacks are tasty as well as healthy. Try some of these:

Boxes with lids
This is a name for tomatoes which have their tops cut off. Hollow them out with a small sharp knife and a spoon, and remove the pips and the juice. But don't throw this away; it can be kept and rubbed through a sieve to make a fresh tomato drink.

You will need large, very sturdy tomatoes, and they can be filled with all kinds of tasty mixtures and then the lids put on top and the filling inside remains a surprise. You can use all sorts of ingredients for the filling, especially left-over cooked foods. Here are a few mixtures:

- Mashed potato, mixed with mashed tinned salmon, mayonnaise and a few left-over peas;
- Little cubes of cheese and cold cooked potato, mixed with mayonnaise and finely chopped parsley;
- Prawns with cubes of cold cooked potato and apple, mixed with mayonnaise;
- Mashed sardines and potato, mixed with mayonnaise and very finely chopped onion;
- Pieces of hardboiled egg, potato cubes and mayonnaise, mixed with finely cut ham and cooked peas;
- Cottage cheese with chives and very finely chopped walnuts;
- Mashed potato with finely chopped gherkins and garlic sausage, mixed with mayonnaise and diced apple;
- Salted herring with potato and onion.

When the tomatoes are filled, replace the lids. Then put them in the refrigerator for at least half an hour to become really cold and refreshing. Using a tube of mayonnaise, squeeze a nice yellow curl on top of each tomato lid. Serve the tomatoes on individual plates or on a serving dish and garnish with fresh, washed lettuce leaves. Serve with toast and butter... it's delicious.

Sandwiches

If you want to make special sandwiches, you can cut away the crusts. Don't throw these crusts away because they can be used to make breadcrumbs or croutons for soup, etc. The slices of bread can now be buttered and spread with the same mixtures already described. The filling should be spread thickly on the slices of bread; at least the same thickness as the bread. You can cool the filling in boxes or bowls in the refrigerator before you use them. As a finishing touch serve the sandwiches wrapped in folded paper serviettes.

Bacon bread

Fry 2 slices of streaky bacon gently in a frying pan. Take some old bread cut in cubes (sandwich crusts) and fry them gently on a low heat, turning them until they are light brown. Then break an egg into a cup, beat it and pour over the top. Sprinkle red paprika powder, chopped chives and marjoram over this. Put the fried bacon slices on top and cook until the egg is set.

Bread should never be wasted; even though ducks and other animals enjoy it, we should still learn to use it up.

Soups

A delicious light soup tastes very good on a cold day, after a brisk walk. Make it with shin of beef cut into small pieces. You will need 200 g/7 oz of meat for 1 litre/1 1/2 pints of soup. Put the meat into cold water and put the pan on a low heat. Simmer for 2-3 hours. Then boil for another 1/2 hour. Add stock cubes. To give more flavour to the soup, add any of the following and simmer for a further 1/2 hour:
- 250 g/8 oz chopped soup vegetables
- Diced celeriac – Diced cucumber – 100 g/4 oz vermicelli or any other small pasta.

Contents